let's cook

rice & risotto

Elizabeth
Wolf-Cohen

p

Contents

Warm Greek-style Rice Salad

This easy-to-make rice salad has all the flavours of the Aegean – olive oil, lemon, feta cheese, capers and tomatoes. It is ideal as an accompaniment to barbecued lamb or chicken.

Serves 4–6

INGREDIENTS

200 g/7 oz/1 cup long-grain white rice
80 ml/3 fl oz/¹⁄₃ cup extra-virgin olive oil
2–3 tbsp lemon juice
1 tbsp chopped fresh oregano or 1 tsp dried oregano
¹⁄₂ tsp Dijon mustard

2 large ripe tomatoes, deseeded and chopped
1 red or green (bell) pepper, deseeded and chopped
75 g/2³⁄₄ oz Kalamata or other brine-cured black olives, stoned (pitted) and halved

225 g/8 oz feta cheese, crumbled, plus extra cubes, to garnish
1 tbsp capers, rinsed and drained
2–4 tbsp chopped fresh flat-leaf parsley or coriander (cilantro)
salt and pepper
diced cucumber, to garnish

1 Bring a saucepan of water to the boil. Add a teaspoon of salt and sprinkle in the rice; return to the boil, stirring once or twice. Reduce the heat and simmer for 15–20 minutes until the rice is tender, stirring once or twice. Drain and rinse under hot running water; drain again.

2 Meanwhile, whisk together the olive oil, lemon juice, oregano, mustard and salt and pepper in a bowl. Add the tomatoes, (bell) pepper, olives, feta cheese, capers and parsley and stir to coat in the dressing. Leave to marinate.

3 Turn the rice into a large bowl; add to the vegetable mixture and toss to mix well.

4 Season the salad with salt and pepper to taste, then divide between 4–6 individual dishes and garnish with extra feta cheese cubes and diced cucumber. Serve just warm.

VARIATION

This salad is also delicious made with brown rice – just increase the cooking time to 25–30 minutes.

Pesto Risotto-rice Salad

This is a cross between a risotto and a rice salad – using Italian arborio rice produces a slightly heavier, stickier result. Substituting long-grain white rice will make a lighter fluffier salad.

Serves 4–6

INGREDIENTS

extra-virgin olive oil
1 onion, finely chopped
200 g/7 oz/1 cup arborio rice
450 ml/16 fl oz/2 cups boiling water
6 sun-dried tomatoes, cut into thin
  slivers
1/2 small red onion, very thinly sliced
3 tbsp lemon juice

PESTO:
50 g/2 oz lightly packed fresh basil
  leaves
2 garlic cloves, finely chopped
2 tbsp pine kernels (nuts), lightly
  toasted
120 ml/4 fl oz/1/2 cup extra-virgin
  olive oil

50 g/1³/₄ oz/¹/₂ cup freshly grated
  Parmesan cheese
salt and pepper

TO GARNISH:
fresh basil leaves
Parmesan shavings

1 To make the pesto, put the basil, garlic and pine kernels (nuts) in a food processor and process for about 30 seconds. With the machine running, gradually pour in the olive oil through the feed tube, until a smooth paste forms. Add the cheese and pulse several times, until blended but still with some texture. Scrape the pesto into a small bowl and season with salt and pepper to taste. Set aside.

2 Heat 1 tablespoon of the oil in a saucepan. Add the onion and cook until beginning to soften. Add the rice and stir to coat. Cook, stirring occasionally, for about 2 minutes. Stir in the boiling water and salt and pepper. Cover and simmer very gently for 20 minutes until the rice is just tender and the water absorbed. Cool slightly.

3 Put the sun-dried tomatoes and sliced onion in a large bowl, add the lemon juice and about 2 tablespoons of oil. Fork in the hot rice and stir in the pesto. Toss to combine. Adjust the seasoning if necessary. Cover and cool to room temperature.

4 Fork the rice mixture into a shallow serving bowl. Drizzle with some olive oil and garnish with basil leaves and Parmesan. Serve the salad at room temperature, not chilled.

Chicken Basquaise

Sweet (bell) peppers are a typical ingredient of dishes from the Basque region in the far West of France. In this recipe, the addition of Bayonne ham, the famous air-dried ham from the Pyrenees, adds a delicious flavour.

Serves 4–5

INGREDIENTS

1.35 kg/3 lb chicken, cut into 8 pieces
flour, for dusting
2–3 tbsp olive oil
1 large onion, (preferably Spanish), thickly sliced
2 (bell) peppers, deseeded and cut lengthways into thick strips
2 garlic cloves

150 g/5 oz spicy chorizo sausage, peeled, if necessary, and cut into 1 cm/¹/₂ inch pieces
1 tbsp tomato purée (paste)
200 g/7 oz/1 cup long-grain white rice or medium-grain Spanish rice, such as valencia
450 ml/16 fl oz/2 cups chicken stock

1 tsp crushed dried chillies
¹/₂ tsp dried thyme
120 g/4 oz Bayonne or other air-dried ham, diced
12 dry-cured black olives
2 tbsp chopped fresh flat-leaf parsley
salt and pepper

1 Dry the chicken pieces well with paper towel. Put about 2 tablespoons flour in a plastic bag, season with salt and pepper and add the chicken pieces. Seal the bag and shake to coat the chicken.

2 Heat 2 tablespoons of the oil in a large flameproof casserole over a medium-high heat. Add the chicken and cook for about 15 minutes until well browned. Transfer to a plate.

3 Heat the remaining oil in the pan and add the onion and (bell) peppers. Reduce the heat to medium and stir-fry until beginning to colour and soften. Add the garlic, chorizo and tomato purée (paste) and continue stirring for about 3 minutes. Add the rice and cook for about 2 minutes, stirring to coat, until the rice is translucent.

4 Add the stock, crushed chillies and thyme and salt and pepper and stir. Bring to the boil. Return the chicken to the pan, pressing gently into the rice. Cover and cook over a very low heat for about 45 minutes until the chicken and rice are tender.

5 Gently stir the ham, black olives and half the parsley into the rice mixture. Re-cover and heat through for a further 5 minutes. Sprinkle with the remaining parsley and serve.

Baked Tomato Rice with Sausages

A great quick supper for the family,
this dish is incredibly simple to put together, yet is truly scrumptious!

Serves 4

INGREDIENTS

2 tbsp vegetable oil
1 onion, coarsely chopped
1 red (bell) pepper, cored, deseeded
  and chopped
2 garlic cloves, finely chopped
½ tsp dried thyme

300 g/10½ oz/1½ cups long-grain
  white rice
1 litre/1¾ pints/4 cups light chicken
  or vegetable stock
225 g/8 oz can chopped tomatoes
1 bay leaf
2 tbsp shredded fresh basil

175 g/6 oz mature (sharp) Cheddar
  cheese, grated
2 tbsp chopped fresh chives
4 herby pork sausages, cooked and cut
  into 1 cm/½ inch pieces
2–3 tbsp freshly grated Parmesan
  cheese

1 Heat the oil in a large flame-proof casserole over medium heat. Add the onion and red (bell) pepper and cook for about 5 minutes, stirring frequently, until soft and lightly coloured. Stir in the garlic and thyme and cook for a further minute.

2 Add the rice and cook, stirring frequently, for about 2 minutes until the rice is well coated and translucent. Stir in the stock, tomatoes and bay leaf. Boil for 5 minutes until the stock is almost absorbed.

3 Stir in the basil, Cheddar cheese, chives and pork sausages and bake, covered, in a preheated oven at 180°C/350°F/Gas Mark 4 for about 25 minutes.

4 Sprinkle with the Parmesan cheese and return to the oven, uncovered, for 5 minutes until the top is golden. Serve hot from the casserole.

VARIATION

For a vegetarian version, replace the pork sausages with a 400 g/14 oz can of drained butter beans, kidney beans, or sweetcorn. Or try a mixture of sautéed mushrooms and courgettes (zucchini).

Seafood Rice

This satisfying rice casserole, bursting with Mediterranean flavours, can be made with any combination of seafood you choose.

Serves 4–6

INGREDIENTS

4 tbsp olive oil

16 large raw peeled prawns (shrimp), tails on if possible

225 g/8 oz cleaned squid or cuttlefish, cut into 1 cm/½ inch slices

2 green (bell) peppers, deseeded and cut lengthways into 1 cm/½ inch strips

1 large onion, finely chopped

4 garlic cloves, finely chopped

2 fresh bay leaves or 1 dried bay leaf

1 tsp saffron threads

½ tsp dried crushed chillies

400 g/14 oz/2 cups arborio or valencia rice

225 ml/8 fl oz/1 cup dry white wine

850 ml/1½ pints /3¾ cups fish, light chicken or vegetable stock

12–16 littleneck clams, well scrubbed

12–16 large mussels, well scrubbed

salt and pepper

2 tbsp chopped fresh flat-leaf parsley, to garnish

RED PEPPER SAUCE:

2–3 tbsp olive oil

2 onions, finely chopped

4–6 garlic cloves, finely chopped

4–6 Italian roasted red (bell) peppers in olive oil (not in vinegar) or roasted, peeled and coarsely chopped

420 g/14½ oz can chopped tomatoes in juice

1–1½ tsp hot paprika

salt

1 To make the red pepper sauce, heat the oil in a saucepan. Add the onions and cook for 6–8 minutes until golden. Stir in the garlic and cook for a minute. Add the remaining ingredients and simmer gently, stirring occasionally, for about 10 minutes. Process to form a smooth sauce; set aside and keep warm.

2 Heat half the oil in a wide pan over a high heat. Add the prawns (shrimp) and stir-fry for 2 minutes until pink. Transfer to a plate. Add the squid and stir-fry for about 2 minutes until just firm. Add to the prawns (shrimp).

3 Heat the remaining oil in the pan, add the green (bell) peppers and onion and stir-fry for about 6 minutes until just tender. Stir in the garlic, bay leaves, saffron and chillies and cook for 30 seconds. Add the rice and cook, stirring, until well coated.

4 Add the wine and stir until absorbed. Add the stock, salt and pepper. Bring to the boil and cover. Simmer gently for about 20 minutes until the rice is just tender and the liquid is almost absorbed.

5 Add the clams and mussels. Re-cover and cook for about 10 minutes until the shells open. Stir in the prawns (shrimp) and squid. Re-cover and heat through. Sprinkle with parsley; serve with the sauce.

Risotto with Cannellini Beans

The Italians, particularly the Tuscans, love dishes made with beans.
This recipe combines beans and rice to make a rich, creamy risotto with a great flavour.

Serves 6–8

INGREDIENTS

300 g/10½ oz cannellini or white
  kidney beans, soaked and cooked
  according to packet instructions
2–3 tbsp olive oil
1 large red (or sweet white) onion,
  finely chopped
3–4 stalks celery, finely chopped

115 g/4 oz pancetta or thick-cut
  smoky bacon
2–3 garlic cloves, minced
¾ tsp dried oregano or 1 tbsp
  chopped fresh oregano
400 g/14 oz/2 cups arborio or
  carnaroli rice

1 litre/1¾ pints/4 cups chicken stock,
  simmering
60 g/2 oz/4 tbsp unsalted butter at
  room temperature
115 g/4 oz/1⅓ cups freshly grated
  Parmesan cheese
salt and pepper

1 Mash, or press through a food mill, half of the cannellini beans and set aside.

2 Heat the olive oil in a large heavy-based saucepan over a medium heat. Add the onion and celery and cook for about 2 minutes until softened. Add the pancetta, garlic and oregano and cook for a further 1–2 minutes, stirring occasionally. Add the rice and cook, stirring frequently, for about 2 minutes until it is translucent and well coated with the oil.

3 Add a ladleful (about 225 ml/ 8 fl oz/1 cup) of the simmering stock; it will bubble and steam rapidly. Cook, stirring constantly, until the stock is absorbed.

4 Continue adding the stock, about half a ladleful at a time, allowing each addition to be absorbed before adding the next. This should take 20–25 minutes.

The risotto should have a creamy consistency and the rice should be tender, but still firm to the bite.

5 Stir in the beans and the bean purée, season with salt and pepper and heat through. Add a little more stock if necessary.

6 Remove from the heat and stir in the butter and half the Parmesan. Cover and stand for about 1 minute. Serve with the remaining Parmesan sprinkled over.

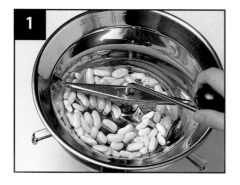

Wild Mushroom Risotto

*Distinctive-tasting wild mushrooms, so popular in Italy,
give this dish a wonderful, robust flavour.*

Serves 6

INGREDIENTS

60 g/2 oz dried porcini or morel
  mushrooms
about 500 g/1 lb 2 oz mixed fresh wild
  mushrooms, such as porcini, girolles,
  horse mushrooms and chanterelles,
  cleaned and halved if large
4 tbsp olive oil

3–4 garlic cloves, finely chopped
60 g/2 oz/4 tbsp unsalted butter
1 onion, finely chopped
350 g/12 oz/1¾ cups arborio or
  carnaroli rice
50 ml/2 fl oz/¼ cup dry white
  vermouth

1.2 litres/2 pints/5 cups chicken stock,
  simmering
115 g/4 oz/1⅓ cups freshly grated
  Parmesan cheese
4 tbsp chopped fresh flat-leaf parsley
salt and pepper

1 Cover the dried mushrooms with boiling water. Leave to soak for 30 minutes, then carefully lift out and pat dry. Strain the soaking liquid through a sieve (strainer) lined with a paper towel, and set aside.

2 Trim the wild mushrooms and gently brush clean.

3 Heat 3 tablespoons of the oil in a large frying pan (skillet) until hot. Add the fresh

mushrooms, and stir-fry for 1–2 minutes. Add the garlic and the soaked mushrooms and cook for 2 minutes, stirring frequently. Scrape on to a plate and set aside.

4 Heat the remaining oil and half the butter in a large heavy-based saucepan. Add the onion and cook for about 2 minutes until softened. Add the rice and cook, stirring frequently, for about 2 minutes until translucent and well coated.

5 Add the vermouth to the rice. When almost absorbed, add a ladleful (about 225 ml/8 fl oz/1 cup) of the simmering stock. Cook, stirring constantly, until the liquid is absorbed.

6 Continue adding the stock, about half a ladleful at a time, allowing each addition to be absorbed before adding the next. This should take 20–25 minutes. The risotto should have a creamy consistency and the rice should be tender, but firm to the bite.

7 Add half the dried mushroom soaking liquid to the risotto and stir in the mushrooms. Season with salt and pepper, and add more mushroom liquid if necessary. Remove from the heat; stir in the remaining butter, Parmesan and parsley. Serve immediately.

Risotto Primavera

This is a nice way to use those first green vegetables which signal the spring, la primavera.
Feel free to add other favourite vegetables, if you like.

Serves 6–8

INGREDIENTS

225 g/8 oz fresh thin asparagus
  spears, well rinsed
4 tbsp olive oil
175 g/6 oz young green beans, cut
  into 2.5 cm/1 inch pieces
175 g/6 oz young courgettes
  (zucchini), quartered and cut into
  2.5 cm/1 inch lengths

225 g/8 oz fresh shelled peas
1 onion, finely chopped
1–2 garlic cloves, finely chopped
350 g/12 oz/1¾ cups arborio or
  carnaroli rice
1.5 litres/2¾ pints/6¼ cups chicken
  stock, simmering, plus extra 2 tbsp

4 spring onions (scallions), cut into
  2.5 cm/1 inch lengths
60 g/2 oz/4 tbsp unsalted butter
115 g/4 oz/1⅓ cups freshly grated
  Parmesan cheese
2 tbsp chopped fresh chives
2 tbsp fresh shredded basil
salt and pepper

1 Trim the woody ends of the asparagus and cut off the tips. Cut the stems into 2.5 cm/1 inch pieces and set aside with the tips.

2 Heat 2 tablespoons of the olive oil in a large frying pan (skillet) over a high heat, until very hot. Add the asparagus, beans, courgettes (zucchini) and peas and stir-fry for 3–4 minutes until they are bright green and just beginning to soften. Set aside.

3 Heat the remaining olive oil in a large heavy-based saucepan over a medium heat. Add the onion and cook for about 1 minute until it begins to soften. Stir in the garlic and cook for 30 seconds. Add the rice and cook, stirring frequently, for 2 minutes until translucent and coated with oil.

4 Add a ladleful (about 225 ml/ 8 fl oz/1 cup) of the hot stock; the stock will bubble rapidly. Cook, stirring constantly, until the stock is absorbed.

5 Continue adding the stock, about half a ladleful at a time, allowing each addition to be absorbed before adding the next – never allow the rice to cook 'dry'. This should take 20–25 minutes. The risotto should have a creamy consistency and the rice should be tender, but firm to the bite.

6 Stir in the stir-fried vegetables and spring onions (scallions) with a little more stock. Cook for 2 minutes, stirring frequently, then season with salt and pepper. Stir in the butter, Parmesan, chives and basil. Remove from the heat, cover and stand for about 1 minute. Garnish with spring onions, if wished. Serve immediately.

Courgette (Zucchini) & Basil Risotto

An easy way of livening up a simple risotto is to use a flavoured olive oil –
here a basil-flavoured oil heightens the taste of the dish.

Serves 4–6

INGREDIENTS

4 tbsp basil-flavoured extra-virgin olive oil, plus extra for drizzling

4 courgettes (zucchini), diced

1 yellow (bell) pepper, cored, deseeded and diced

2 garlic cloves, finely chopped

1 large onion, finely chopped

400 g/14 oz/2 cups arborio or carnaroli rice

60 ml/3 fl oz/⅓ cup dry white vermouth

1.5 litres/2¾ pints/6¼ cups chicken or vegetable stock, simmering

25 g/1 oz/2 tbsp unsalted butter, at room temperature

large handful of fresh basil leaves, torn, plus a few leaves to garnish

80 g/3 oz/1 cup freshly grated Parmesan cheese

1 Heat half the oil in a large frying pan (skillet) over high heat. When very hot, but not smoking, add the courgettes (zucchini) and yellow (bell) pepper and stir-fry for 3 minutes until lightly golden. Stir in the garlic and cook for about 30 seconds longer. Transfer to a plate and set aside.

2 Heat the remaining oil in a large heavy-based saucepan over a medium heat. Add the chopped onion and cook for about 2 minutes until softened. Add the rice and cook, stirring frequently, for about 2 minutes until the rice is translucent and well coated with the oil.

3 Pour in the vermouth; it will bubble and steam rapidly and evaporate almost immediately. Add a ladleful (about 225 ml/8 fl oz/1 cup) of the simmering stock and cook, stirring constantly until the stock is absorbed.

4 Continue adding the stock, about half a ladleful at a time, allowing each addition to be absorbed before adding the next. This should take 20–25 minutes. The risotto should have a creamy consistency and the rice should be tender, but still firm to the bite.

5 Stir in the courgette (zucchini) mixture with any juices, the butter, basil and Parmesan. Drizzle with a little oil and garnish with basil. Serve hot.

Wild Rocket (Arugula) & Tomato Risotto with Mozzarella

It's worth searching around for wild rocket as its robust peppery flavour makes all the difference to this dish. Teamed with vine-ripened plum tomatoes and real buffalo mozzarella, this risotto is sensational.

Serves 4–6

INGREDIENTS

2 tbsp olive oil
25 g/1 oz/2 tbsp unsalted butter
1 large onion, finely chopped
2 garlic cloves, finely chopped
350 g/12 oz/1¾ cups arborio rice
120 ml/4 fl oz/½ cup dry white
    vermouth (optional)

1.5 litres/2¾ pints/6¼ cups chicken
    or vegetable stock, simmering
6 vine-ripened or Italian plum
    tomatoes, deseeded and chopped
125 g/4½ oz wild rocket (arugula)
handful of fresh basil leaves

115 g/4 oz/1⅓ cups freshly grated
    Parmesan cheese
225 g/8 oz fresh Italian buffalo
    mozzarella, coarsely grated or diced
salt and pepper

1 Heat the oil and half the butter in a large frying pan (skillet). Add the onion and cook for about 2 minutes until just beginning to soften. Stir in the garlic and rice and cook, stirring frequently, until the rice is translucent and well coated.

2 Pour in the white vermouth, if using; it will bubble and steam rapidly and evaporate almost immediately. Add a ladleful (about 225 ml/8 fl oz/1 cup) of the simmering stock and cook, stirring constantly, until it is absorbed.

3 Continue adding the stock, about half a ladleful at a time, allowing each addition to be absorbed before adding the next – never allow the rice to cook 'dry'.

4 Just before the rice is tender, stir in the chopped tomatoes and rocket (arugula). Shred the basil leaves and immediately stir into the risotto. Continue to cook, adding more stock, until the risotto is creamy and the rice is tender, but firm to the bite.

5 Remove from the heat and stir in the remaining butter, the Parmesan and mozzarella. Season to taste with salt and pepper. Cover and stand for about 1 minute. Serve immediately, before the mozzarella melts completely.

Crab Risotto with Roasted (Bell) Peppers

A different way to make the most of crab,
this rich-tasting and colourful risotto is full of interesting flavours.

Serves 4–6

INGREDIENTS

2–3 large red (bell) peppers
3 tbsp olive oil
1 onion, finely chopped
1 small fennel bulb, finely chopped
2 stalks celery, finely chopped
1/4–1/2 tsp cayenne pepper, or to taste

350 g/12 oz/1³/₄ cups arborio or
  carnaroli rice
800 g/1 lb 12 oz can Italian peeled
  plum tomatoes, drained and
  chopped
50 ml/2 fl oz/¹/₄ cup dry white
  vermouth (optional)

1.5 litres/2³/₄ pints/6¹/₄ cups fish or
  light chicken stock, simmering
450 g/1 lb fresh cooked crab meat
  (white and dark meat)
50 ml/2 fl oz/¹/₄ cup lemon juice
2–4 tbsp chopped fresh parsley or chervil
salt and pepper

1 Grill (broil) the (bell) peppers until the skins are charred. Transfer to a plastic bag and twist to seal. When cool enough to handle, peel off the charred skins, working over a bowl to catch the juices. Remove the cores and seeds; chop the flesh and set aside, reserving the juices.

2 Heat the olive oil in a large heavy-based saucepan. Add the onion, fennel and celery and cook for 2–3 minutes until the

vegetables are softened. Add the cayenne and rice and cook, stirring frequently, for about 2 minutes until the rice is translucent and well coated.

3 Stir in the tomatoes and vermouth, if using. The liquid will bubble and steam rapidly. When the liquid is almost absorbed, add a ladleful (about 225 ml/8 fl oz/ 1 cup) of the simmering stock. Cook, stirring constantly, until the liquid is completely absorbed.

4 Continue adding the stock, about half a ladleful at a time, allowing each addition to be absorbed before adding the next. This should take 20–25 minutes. The risotto should have a creamy consistency and the rice should be tender, but firm to the bite.

5 Stir in the red (bell) peppers and juices, the crab meat, lemon juice and parsley or chervil and heat. Season with salt and pepper to taste. Serve immediately.

Arrancini

*These little risotto-ball snacks are as popular in New York as they are in Rome.
The mozzarella centres ooze deliciously when you bite into them.*

Serves 6–8

INGREDIENTS

1 quantity Risotto alla Milanese
  (page 32), completely cooled
3 eggs
3 tbsp chopped fresh flat-leaf parsley

115 g/4 oz/²⁄₃ cup mozzarella, diced
vegetable oil, for frying
about 80 g/3 oz/²⁄₃ cup plain
  (all-purpose) flour

about 100 g/3¹⁄₂ oz/l¹⁄₂ cups dried
  breadcrumbs, preferably homemade
salt and pepper

---

1 Put the risotto in a large mixing bowl and stir to break up. Beat 2 of the eggs lightly, then gradually beat enough into the risotto until the risotto begins to stick together. Beat in the parsley.

2 Using wet hands, form the mixture into balls about the size of a large egg.

3 Poke a hole in the centre of each ball and fill with a few cubes of the mozzarella. Carefully seal the hole over with the risotto mixture. Place on a large baking (cookie) sheet.

4 In a deep-fat fryer or large heavy-based saucepan, heat about 7.5 cm/3 inches of oil to 180–190°C/350-375°F or until a cube of bread browns.

5 Spread the flour on a large plate and season with salt and pepper. In a small bowl, beat the remaining egg and add any unused egg from Step 1. Spread the breadcrumbs on another large plate and season with salt and pepper.

6 Roll each risotto ball in a little seasoned flour, shaking off the excess. Carefully coat in the egg, then roll in the breadcrumbs to coat completely.

7 Deep fry 3–4 balls for about 2 minutes until crisp and golden, then transfer to paper towels to drain. Keep hot in a warm oven while frying the remaining balls. Serve immediately while the cheese is still soft and melted.

Frittata Risotto

*An excellent way of using up leftover risotto, this fried risotto 'cake' makes a great first course,
or a tasty accompaniment to roasted or grilled (broiled) meats.*

Serves 4–6

INGREDIENTS

about 80 ml/3 fl oz/⅓ cup olive oil
1 large red onion, finely chopped
1 red (bell) pepper, cored, deseeded
  and chopped
1 garlic clove, finely chopped

3–4 sun-dried tomatoes, finely
  shredded
2 tbsp chopped fresh flat-leaf parsley
  or basil

1 quantity Risotto alla Milanese (see
  page 32), cooled
about 60 g/2 oz/⅔ cup freshly grated
  Parmesan cheese

1 Heat 2 tablespoons of the oil in a large heavy-based frying pan (skillet) over a medium-high heat. Add the onion and red (bell) pepper and cook for 3–4 minutes until the vegetables are soft.

2 Add the garlic and sun-dried tomatoes and cook for 2 minutes. Remove from the heat. Stir in the parsley; cool slightly.

3 Put the risotto in a bowl and break up with a fork. Stir in the vegetable mixture with half the Parmesan. Stir to mix well.

4 Reserve 1 tablespoon of the remaining oil and heat the rest in the cleaned frying pan (skillet) over a medium heat. Remove from the heat and spoon in the risotto mixture, pressing it into an even cake-like layer, about 2–2.5 cm/¾–1 inch thick. Return to the heat and cook for about 4 minutes until crisp and brown on the bottom.

5 With a palette knife, loosen the edges and give the pan a shake. Slide the frittata on to a large plate. Protecting your hands, invert the frying pan (skillet) over the frittata and, holding both firmly together, flip them over. Return to the heat and drizzle the remaining oil around the edge of the frittata, gently pulling the edges towards the centre with the palette knife. Cook for 1–2 minutes to seal the bottom, then slide on to a serving plate.

6 Sprinkle the top with some of the remaining Parmesan. Cut into wedges and serve with the rest of the Parmesan.

Oven-baked Risotto with Mushrooms

*This easy-to-make risotto is a good choice for entertaining as it eliminates the need
for constant stirring. The result is creamy and moist – more like a rice pudding.*

Serves 4–6

INGREDIENTS

4 tbsp olive oil
400 g/14 oz portobello or large field
   mushrooms, thickly sliced
115 g/4 oz pancetta or thick-cut
   smoky bacon, diced
1 large onion, finely chopped

2 garlic cloves, finely chopped
350 g/12 oz/1¾ cups arborio or
   carnaroli rice
1.2 litres/2 pints/5 cups chicken stock,
   simmering

2 tbsp chopped fresh tarragon or flat-
   leaf parsley
80 g/3 oz/1 cup freshly grated
   Parmesan cheese, plus extra for
   sprinkling
salt and pepper

1 Heat 2 tablespoons of the oil in a large heavy-based frying pan (skillet) over a high heat. Add the mushrooms and stir-fry for 2–3 minutes until golden and tender-crisp. Transfer to a plate.

2 Add the pancetta to the pan and cook for about 2 minutes, stirring frequently, until crisp and golden. Add to the mushrooms on the plate.

3 Heat the remaining oil in a heavy-based saucepan over a medium heat. Add the onion and cook for about 2 minutes until beginning to soften. Add the garlic and rice and cook, stirring, for about 2 minutes until the rice is well coated with the oil.

4 Gradually stir the stock into the rice, then add the mushroom and pancetta mixture and the tarragon. Season with salt and pepper. Bring to the boil.

5 Remove from the heat and transfer to a casserole.

6 Cover and bake in a preheated oven at 180°C/350°F/Gas Mark 4 for about 20 minutes until the rice is almost tender and most of the liquid is absorbed. Uncover and stir in the Parmesan. Continue to bake for about 15 minutes longer until the rice is tender, but still firm to the bite. Serve at once with extra Parmesan for sprinkling.

Risotto alla Milanese

*This risotto, traditionally served as an accompaniment to Ossobuco alla Milanese,
is one of the world's most beautiful and elegant dishes.*

Serves 4–6

INGREDIENTS

½–1 tsp saffron threads
1.3 litres/2¼ pints/5⅔ cups chicken
   stock, simmering
80 g/3 oz/6 tbsp unsalted butter

2–3 shallots, finely chopped
400 g/14 oz/2 cups arborio or
   carnaroli rice

175 g/6 oz/2 cups freshly grated
   Parmesan cheese
salt and pepper

1 Put the saffron threads in a small bowl. Pour over enough of the stock to cover the threads, then set aside to infuse.

2 Melt 25 g/1 oz/2 tablespoons of the butter in a large heavy-based pan over a medium heat. Add the shallots and cook for about 2 minutes until beginning to soften. Add the rice and cook, stirring frequently, for about 2 minutes until the rice is beginning to turn translucent and is well coated.

3 Add a ladleful (about 225 ml/8 fl oz/1 cup) of the simmering stock; it will steam and bubble rapidly. Cook, stirring constantly, until the liquid is absorbed.

4 Continue adding the stock, about half a ladleful at a time, allowing each addition to be absorbed before adding the next – never allow the rice to cook 'dry'.

5 After about 15 minutes, stir in the saffron-infused stock; the rice will turn a vibrant yellow and the colour will become deeper as it cooks. Continue cooking, adding the stock in the same way until the rice is tender, but still firm to the bite. The risotto should have a creamy porridge-like consistency.

6 Stir in the remaining butter and half the Parmesan, then remove from the heat. Cover and stand for about 1 minute.

7 Spoon the risotto into serving bowls and serve immediately with the remaining Parmesan.

Dolmades

These stuffed grape-vine leaves are popular all over the Middle-East, where they are served as part of a meze – a selection of appetizers. This is a simple rice version.

Serves 10–12

INGREDIENTS

115 g/4 oz/about 24 large vine leaves, packed in brine, drained
olive oil
1 onion, finely chopped
2 garlic cloves, finely chopped
³/₄ tsp dried thyme
³/₄ tsp dried oregano

¹/₂ tsp ground cinnamon
200 g/7 oz/1 cup long-grain white rice
350 ml/12 fl oz/1¹/₂ cups water
2 tsp raisins
2 tbsp pine kernels (nuts), lightly toasted
2 tbsp chopped fresh mint

1 tbsp chopped fresh flat-leaf parsley
4 tbsp lemon juice
350 ml/12 fl oz/1¹/₂ cups chicken stock
salt and pepper

1 Cover the vine leaves with boiling water and leave for 2 minutes. Drain, rinse and pat dry. Cut off any thick stems. Place shiny-side down on paper towels.

2 Heat 2 tablespoons of the olive oil in a heavy-based pan. Add the onion and cook for about 3 minutes until soft. Stir in the garlic, dried herbs and cinnamon, then add the rice and cook for about 2 minutes, stirring, until translucent and coated with the oil.

3 Stir in the water and raisins and bring to the boil, stirring twice. Simmer, covered tightly, for 15 minutes until the liquid is absorbed and the rice just tender.

4 Fork the rice into a bowl and add the pine kernels (nuts), mint, parsley and half the lemon juice. Stir and season with salt and pepper and 1 tablespoon olive oil.

5 Place about 1 tablespoon of the rice mixture on a vine leaf near the stem end and roll the leaf once over the filling. Fold in each side of the leaf, then finish rolling. Repeat with the remaining leaves.

6 Brush a large deep flameproof dish or casserole with about 2 tablespoons of olive oil. Arrange the dolmades tightly in 2 rows, making a second layer if necessary. Sprinkle with another tablespoon of the oil and the remaining lemon juice. Add the stock to cover the rolls; add extra water if necessary to make enough liquid.

7 Weight down the rolls with a heatproof plate, cover tightly with a lid or kitchen foil and cook over a very low heat for about 1 hour. Remove from the heat and allow to cool to room temperature. Drain and serve with a little of the cooking juices, if wished.

Kedgeree

Originally served at Victorian breakfast tables, kedgeree probably derives from an Indian dish called khichri. The strong flavour of the smoked fish is a perfect match for the blandness of rice.

Serves 4–6

INGREDIENTS

700 g/1½ lb thick, undyed smoked
   haddock or cod fillets
milk, for poaching
2 bay leaves
1 tbsp vegetable oil
60 g/2 oz/4 tbsp butter
1 onion, finely chopped

1 tsp hot curry powder, or to taste
1 tsp dry mustard powder
300 g/10½ oz/1½ cups basmati rice
750 ml/1⅓ pints/3½ cups water
2 small leeks, trimmed and cut into 5
   mm/¼ inch slices

2 tbsp chopped fresh flat-leaf parsley
   or coriander (cilantro)
a squeeze of lemon juice
3–4 hard-boiled (hard-cooked) eggs,
   peeled and quartered
salt and pepper
lemon quarters, to serve

1 Put the fish in a frying pan (skillet) and pour in enough milk to just cover; add the bay leaves. Bring to the boil, then simmer gently, covered, for about 4 minutes. Remove from the heat and stand, covered, for about 10 minutes.

2 Using a slotted spoon, transfer the fish to a plate and cover loosely; set aside. Reserve the cooking milk, discarding the bay leaves.

3 Heat the oil and half the butter in a large pan over a medium heat. Add the onion and cook for about 2 minutes until soft. Stir in the curry powder and the mustard powder and cook for 1 minute.

4 Add the rice and stir for about 2 minutes until well coated. Add the water and bring to the boil; stir and reduce the heat to very low. Cook, covered, for 20–25 minutes until the rice is tender and the water absorbed.

5 Melt the remaining butter in a flameproof casserole, add the leeks and cook for about 4 minutes until soft. Fork the leeks into the hot rice. Add 2–3 tablespoons of the reserved milk to moisten.

6 Flake the fish off the skin into large pieces and fold into the rice. Stir in the parsley and lemon juice, then season with salt and pepper. Add a little more milk, if wished, then add the egg quarters. Serve, with lemon quarters.

Spanish Paella

This classic recipe gets its name from the wide metal pan traditionally used for cooking the dish – a paellera.

Serves 4

INGREDIENTS

120 ml/4 fl oz/½ cup olive oil
1.5 kg/3 lb 5 oz chicken, cut into 8 pieces
350 g/12 oz chorizo sausage, cut into 1 cm/½ inch pieces
115 g/4 oz cured ham, chopped
2 onions, finely chopped
2 red (bell) peppers, cored, deseeded and cut into 2.5 cm/1 inch pieces

4–6 garlic cloves
750 g/1 lb 10 oz/3¾ cups short-grain Spanish rice or Italian arborio rice
2 bay leaves
1 tsp dried thyme
1 tsp saffron threads, lightly crushed
225 ml/8 fl oz/1 cup dry white wine
1.5 litres/2¾ pints/6¼ cups chicken stock

115 g/4 oz fresh shelled or defrosted frozen peas
450 g/1 lb medium uncooked prawns (shrimp)
8 raw King prawns (shrimp), in shells
16 clams, very well scrubbed
16 mussels, very well scrubbed
salt and pepper
4 tbsp chopped fresh flat-leaf parsley

1 Heat half the oil in a 46 cm/ 18 inch paella pan or deep, wide frying pan (skillet) over a medium-high heat. Add the chicken and fry gently, turning, until golden brown. Remove from the pan and set aside.

2 Add the chorizo and ham to the pan and cook for about 7 minutes, stirring occasionally, until crisp. Remove and set aside.

3 Stir the onions into the pan and cook for about 3 minutes until soft. Add the (bell) peppers and garlic and cook until beginning to soften; remove and set aside.

4 Add the remaining oil to the pan and stir in the rice until well coated. Add the bay leaves, thyme and saffron and stir well. Pour in the wine, bubble, then pour in the stock, stirring well and

scraping the bottom of the pan. Bring to the boil, stirring often.

5 Stir in the cooked vegetables. Add the chorizo, ham and chicken and gently bury in the rice. Reduce the heat and cook for 10 minutes, stirring occasionally.

6 Add the peas and prawns (shrimp) and cook for a further 5 minutes. Push the clams and mussels into the rice. Cover and cook over a very low heat for about 5 minutes until the rice is tender and the shellfish open. Discard any unopened clams or mussels. Season to taste.

7 Remove from heat, and stand, covered, for about 5 minutes. Sprinkle with parsley and serve.

Mediterranean Stuffed Peppers

Serve the (bell) peppers with their tops for an attractive finish – blanch them with the peppers,
then bake separately for the last 10 minutes and place in position just before serving.

Serves 6

INGREDIENTS

6 large (bell) peppers, red, yellow and
  orange
200 g/7 oz/1 cup long-grain white rice
2–3 tbsp olive oil, plus extra for
  greasing and drizzling
1 large onion
2 stalks celery, chopped

2 garlic cloves, finely chopped
$\frac{1}{2}$ tsp ground cinnamon or allspice
75 g/2$\frac{3}{4}$ oz/$\frac{1}{2}$ cup raisins
4 tbsp pine kernels (nuts), lightly
  toasted
4 ripe plum tomatoes, deseeded and
  chopped

50 ml/2 fl oz/$\frac{1}{4}$ cup white wine
4 anchovy fillets, chopped
$\frac{1}{2}$ bunch chopped fresh parsley
$\frac{1}{2}$ bunch chopped fresh mint
6 tbsp freshly grated Parmesan cheese
salt and pepper
fresh tomato sauce, to serve (optional)

1 Using a sharp knife, slice off the tops of the (bell) peppers, then remove the cores and seeds. Blanch the (bell) peppers in boiling water for 2–3 minutes. Carefully remove and drain upside-down on a wire rack.

2 Bring a saucepan of salted water to the boil. Gradually pour in the rice and return to the boil; simmer until tender, but firm to the bite. Drain and rinse under cold running water. Set aside.

3 Heat the oil in a large frying pan (skillet). Add the onion and celery and cook for 2 minutes. Stir in the garlic, cinnamon and raisins and cook for 1 minute. Fork in the rice, then stir in the pine kernels (nuts), tomatoes, wine, anchovies, parsley and mint and cook for 4 minutes. Remove from the heat, add salt and pepper and stir in half the Parmesan.

4 Brush the bottom of a baking dish with a little oil. Divide the rice mixture equally among the peppers. Arrange in the dish and sprinkle with the remaining Parmesan. Drizzle with a little more oil and pour in enough water to come 1 cm/$\frac{1}{2}$ inch up the sides of the peppers. Loosely cover the dish with kitchen foil.

5 Bake in a preheated oven at 180°C/350°F/Gas Mark 4 for about 40 minutes. Uncover and cook for a further 10 minutes. Serve hot with tomato sauce.

Creole Jambalaya

A rich, rice-based stew, combining a fabulous mix of meat and seafood with exciting peppery flavourings, Jambalaya captures the true essence of Creole cooking.

Serves 6–8

INGREDIENTS

2 tbsp vegetable oil
80 g/3 oz piece good-quality smoked ham, cut into bite-sized pieces
80 g/3 oz/½ cup andouille or pure smoked pork sausage, such as Polish kielbasa, cut into chunks
2 large onions, finely chopped
3–4 stalks celery, finely chopped
2 green (bell) peppers, cored, deseeded and finely chopped
2 garlic cloves, finely chopped

225 g/8 oz boned chicken breast or thighs, skinned and cut into pieces
4 ripe tomatoes, skinned and chopped
175 ml/6 fl oz/¾ cup passata or sieved strained tomatoes
450 ml/16 fl oz/2 cups fish stock
400 g/14 oz/2 cups long-grain white rice
4 spring onions (scallions), cut into 2.5 cm/1 inch pieces
250 g/9 oz peeled raw prawns (shrimp), tails on, if wished

250 g/9 oz cooked white crab meat
12 oysters, shelled (shucked), with their liquor

SEASONING MIX:
2 dried bay leaves
1 tsp salt
1½–2 tsp cayenne pepper, or to taste
1½ tsp dried oregano
1 tsp ground white pepper, or to taste
1 tsp black pepper, or to taste

1 To make the seasoning mix, mix the ingredients in a bowl.

2 Heat the oil in a flameproof casserole over a medium heat. Add the smoked ham and the sausage and cook for about 8 minutes, stirring frequently, until golden. Using a slotted spoon, transfer to a large plate.

3 Add the onions, celery and (bell) peppers to the casserole and cook for about 4 minutes until just softened. Stir in the garlic, then remove and set aside.

4 Add the chicken pieces to the casserole and cook for 3–4 minutes until beginning to colour. Stir in the seasoning mix to coat.

5 Return the ham, sausage and vegetables to the casserole and stir to combine. Add the chopped tomatoes and passata, then pour in the stock. Bring to the boil.

6 Stir in the rice and reduce the heat to a simmer. Cook for about 12 minutes. Uncover, stir in the spring onions (scallions) and prawns (shrimp) and cook, covered, for 4 minutes.

7 Add the crab meat and oysters with their liquor and gently stir in. Cook until the rice is just tender, and the oysters slightly firm. Remove from the heat and leave to stand, covered, for about 3 minutes before serving.

Lamb Biriyani

For an authentic finishing touch, garnish with crisply-fried onion rings,
toasted slivered almonds, chopped pistachio nuts and pieces of edible silver foil (vark).

Serves 6–8

INGREDIENTS

900 g/2 lb boned lean leg or shoulder of lamb, cut into 2.5 cm/1 inch cubes
6 garlic cloves, finely chopped
4 cm/1½ inch piece fresh ginger root, peeled and finely chopped
1 tbsp ground cinnamon
1 tbsp green cardamom pods, crushed to expose the black seeds
1 tsp whole cloves
2 tsp coriander seeds, crushed

2 tsp cumin seeds, crushed
½ tsp ground turmeric (optional)
2 fresh green chillies, deseeded and chopped
grated rind and juice of 1 lime
1 bunch fresh coriander (cilantro), chopped finely
1 bunch fresh mint, chopped finely
120 ml/4 fl oz/½ cup natural yogurt
115 g/4 oz/8 tbsp ghee, butter or vegetable oil

4 onions, 3 thinly sliced and 1 finely chopped
600 g/1 lb 5 oz/3 cups basmati rice
2 cinnamon sticks, broken
½ a whole nutmeg, freshly grated
3–4 tbsp raisins
1.2 litres/2 pints/5 cups chicken stock or water
225 ml/8 fl oz/1 cup hot milk
1 tsp saffron threads, slightly crushed
salt and pepper

1 Combine the lamb with the garlic, ginger, cinnamon, cardamom, cloves, coriander and cumin seeds, turmeric, chillies, lime rind and juice, 2 tablespoons each of coriander and mint and yogurt. Marinate for 2–3 hours.

2 Heat about half the fat in a large frying pan (skillet), add the sliced onions and cook for about 8 minutes until lightly browned. Add the meat and any juices; season with salt and pepper. Stir in about 225 ml/8 fl oz/1 cup water and simmer for 18–20 minutes until the lamb is just cooked.

3 Meanwhile, heat the fat left over in a flameproof casserole. Add the chopped onion and cook for 2 minutes until soft. Add the rice and cook, stirring, for 3–4 minutes until well coated. Add the cinnamon, nutmeg, raisins and stock. Bring to the boil, stirring once or twice, and season with salt and pepper. Simmer, covered, over a low heat for 12 minutes until the liquid is reduced but the rice is still a little firm.

4 Pour the hot milk over the saffron; stand for 10 minutes. Remove the rice from the heat and stir in the saffron-milk. Fold in the lamb mixture. Cover and bake in a preheated oven at 350°C/180°F/Gas Mark 4 until the rice is cooked and the liquid absorbed.

Chinese Fried Rice

This simple Cantonese recipe for using leftover rice has become a world-wide speciality in Chinese restaurants. Enjoy this homemade version, which includes ham and prawns (shrimp).

Serves 4–6

INGREDIENTS

2–3 tbsp groundnut or vegetable oil
2 onions, halved and cut lengthways
   into thin wedges
2 garlic cloves, thinly sliced
2.5 cm/1 inch piece fresh ginger root,
   peeled, sliced and cut into slivers
200 g/7 oz cooked ham, thinly sliced

750 g/1 lb 10 oz/4 cups cooked, cold
   long-grain white rice
250 g/9 oz cooked peeled prawns (shrimp)
115 g/4 oz canned water chestnuts, sliced
3 eggs
3 tsp sesame oil

4–6 spring onions (scallions), diagonally
   sliced into 2.5 cm/1 inch pieces
2 tbsp dark soy sauce or Thai fish sauce
1 tbsp sweet chilli sauce
2 tbsp chopped fresh coriander (cilantro)
   or flat-leaf parsley
salt and pepper

1 Heat 2–3 tablespoons groundnut oil in a wok or large, deep frying pan (skillet) until very hot. Add the onions and stir-fry for about 2 minutes until beginning to soften. Add the garlic and ginger and stir-fry for another minute. Add the ham strips and stir to combine.

2 Add the cold cooked rice and stir to mix with the vegetables and ham. Stir in the prawns (shrimp) and the water

chestnuts. Stir in 2 tablespoons water and cover the pan quickly. Continue to cook for 2 minutes, shaking the pan occasionally to prevent sticking and to allow the rice to heat through.

3 Beat the eggs with 1 teaspoon of the sesame oil and season with salt and pepper. Make a well in the centre of the rice mixture, add the eggs and immediately stir, gradually drawing the rice into the eggs.

4 Stir in the spring onions (scallions), soy sauce and chilli sauce and stir-fry; stir in a little more water if the rice looks dry or is sticking. Drizzle in the remaining sesame oil and stir. Season to taste with salt and pepper.

5 Remove from the heat, wipe the edge of the wok or frying pan (skillet) and sprinkle with the coriander (cilantro). Serve immediately from the pan.

This is a Parragon Book
First published in 2003

Parragon
Queen Street House
4 Queen Street, Bath, BA1 1HE, UK

ISBN: 1-40540-833-2

Printed in China

NOTE

This book uses imperial and metric measurements. Follow the same units
of measurement throughout; do not mix imperial and metric. All spoon
measurements are level; teaspoons are assumed to be 5 ml and
tablespoons are assumed to be 15 ml. Unless otherwise stated, milk is
assumed to be whole milk, eggs and individual vegetables such as
potatoes are medium, and pepper is freshly ground black pepper.

The times given for each recipe are an approximate guide only because
the preparation times may differ according to the techniques used by
different people and the cooking times may vary as a result of the type of
oven used.

Recipes using raw or very lightly cooked eggs should be avoided by
infants, the elderly, pregnant women, convalescents and anyone suffering
from an illness.